Money and Abundance

The Main Key to Making a Decision

TABLE OF CONTENTS

INTRODUCTION

It does not matter which part of the world you're living in, the importance attached to money is both universal and conventional. The poor wants to get rich, the rich aims to getting richer: Well, no surprise Steve Martin once said, "I love money, I love everything about it. I bought some pretty good stuff, Got me a $300 pair of socks. Got a fur sink, An electric dog polisher. A gasoline powered turtleneck sweater. And, of course, I bought some useful stuff, too."

Just as you might have possibly known from way back, for any commodity to be referred to as money, it must be durable, it must be divisible, it must be acceptable, it must be portable, it must be uniform and must be limited in supply.

The history of money dates back to several decades ago. Initially, there were different forms of exchange by barter going on in the world, which is a form of buying and selling between two people or even more.

However, the term "Currency" has ever since been a means to an end; a measure of the particular identity and value that different forms of money entails all over the world.

Over the ages, Different forms of money have been invented . But In the year 1690, Massachusetts Bay Colony issued the first paper money in the U.S. Ever since, money has become a much needed essential everywhere.

Though, a happy day comes with the abundance of money, are you willing to go all out to work hard for it? Are you going to pursue your dream of becoming a millionaire or billionaire at a certain age with rigor and strength? Are you willing to sacrifice your time and concentration for it? Then the question is; why do people fail to have money in abundance? Why many people fail to have money in abundance is because they do not want to work hard to have money based on the efforts or price needed to be paid into having it. Talking about most successful people in the world today, we can deduce that they are the set of people who work very hard for their money. They have principles which guides them on their way to becoming the richest people in the world.

In this book, you shall be exposed to more money and the principles which makes the rich gets richer and the poor gets poorer or even less.

CHAPTER ONE

HAVING MONEY IS ESSENTIAL

There is a poor man down the street who hardly earns a dollar in a whole day. He lives in sorrow and regrets everyday the sun shines on his face. He is unable to sit with the big wigs of the society. He is not able to afford the good things of life; including good food, good shelter, good association and not only those: he is unable to command respect whenever he gets to a new place or opens his mouth to talk.

Why do you think this man has to go through all these ordeals? Your guess is as good as mine. He does not have money!

Money has its own way of giving you comfort. The consciousness that a good amount of money is sitting in your bank account would always give a great feeling on it's own.

Having money in abundance in our world today is termed "Abundance of Wealth." Wealth, according to the English dictionary is defined as a great amount; an abundance or plenty. It is possible to have wealth in terms of knowledge, wealth in terms of good health, and wealth in terms of money. All of these are good and very essential to a happy living in this world. It is however true that most of us desire to have money in abundance. There is absolutely no one in the world who doesn't want to be termed "wealthy" with relations to money, we literarily want to be able to buy whatever we want with the fat amount of money sitting comfortably in our bank accounts each passing day. The former U.S President, Barrack Obama, puts it like this: "Money is not the only answer, but it makes a difference." Bo Dereck has this to say, "Whoever said money can't buy happiness simply didn't know where to go shopping." wow! This can be one of the best ways to putting it right.

The need to have money is an insatiable one, implying the fact that it cannot be satisfied. Both the young and the old, the rich and the poor, the leader and the follower, the sick and the strong, are all in the deep search for money in order to satisfy their infallible thirst for the good things of life. To the sick, money is essential for medical treatment or surgery. To the rich, money is essential for sending their wards to the best Universities in the country or even abroad. To the average person, money is essential for acquiring the basic needs of life. Indeed, the importance of money in the lives of each individuals in the world cannot be over-emphasized.

CHAPTER TWO

IS IT A CRIME TO WANT MONEY IN ABUNDANCE?

Absolutely no! Wanting to have money in abundance is a very good trait. Henry David Thoreau puts it like this, "Wealth is the ability to experience life." In order to truly experience how marvelous and sweet the good things of life are, then being wealthy is the state that you want to be. It is as simple as that.

People who only want to live an average life are the ones who do not desire to have money in abundance. They are the set of people who celebrate mediocrity. They are the set of people who would glory in having a little dollars in their pocket and nothing in their bank accounts all the days of their lives. They are the set of people who are lazy and would prefer to beg the rich people in their neighborhood to borrow them money or donate money to them freely. Successful people do not have such bad traits. Wealthy people are those who always want money, and they want it in abundance.

An anonymous quote once said, "Rule number one: Have money in abundance. Rule number two: always repeat number one." The key to having an abundance of wealth is in learning the principles which makes you to always have money. People who do not learn these principles are often confined to the gutter of mediocrity and poor living. Successful people know how to recycle their wealth, wealthy people always learn to spend their money on things that would bring back even more money to them. These set of people do not see having money in abundance as a crime, they always want to have more money every single day of their life.

It is not only necessary but compulsory that you move away from people who make you feel like your desire for money is a bad thing. More often, These kinds of people leaves you with the impression like it is such a big crime to chase wealth. There is no need for any soothsayer to attest to the fact that such people are toxic to your destiny. They will always want you be in the mediocre level that they have found themselves. Even if such people are rich, it is still good that you move away from such people. You can ask yourself; how did they find themselves in their rich and wealthy state if having money in abundance is a crime or a bad thing? Oops!

CHAPTER THREE

YOUR PAST DOESN'T MATTER!

To become wealthy and have money in abundance, your past doesn't matter. In the famous book: Purpose Driven life, Rick Warren highlighted clearly, "We are products of our past, but we don't have to be prisoners to it." It truly does not matter where you are coming from or where you are currently; rather, in order to possess money in abundance, what matters most is striving to the wealthy state you have always dreamt of reaching in life.

A big notable mistake passed across generations is feeling contented with an average life. Beryl Markham once said, "I have learned that if you must leave a place that you have lived in and loved and where all your yesteryears are buried deeply, leave it any way except a slow way, leave it the fastest way you can. Never turn back and never believe that an hour you remember is a better hour because it is dead. Passed years seem safe ones, vanquished ones, while the future lives in a cloud, formidable from a distance."

Many of us have allowed our circumstances, family background, education history, past events in our lives, to hold us down from achieving our dreams. Willingly or unwillingly, some people have allowed the bad spells which they went through to confine themselves to the level of mediocrity. Gautama Buddha puts it like this, "No one saves us but ourselves. No one can and no one may. We ourselves must work the path. In his book titled: "Unexpected Blessings", Barbara Taylor Bradford said, " The past was always there, lived inside of you, and it helped to make you who you were. But it had to be placed in perspective. The past could not dominate the future." Those who make their past their best friends are those who do not end up getting whatever they wanted from life.

Establishing that your past failures and past horrible experiences in life do not determine the heights you can reach in life is the best way to begin your journey towards having money in abundance. Many of the successful people in our world today are people who could go on and on about their mediocre past. At the end of the day, they'd have spent vast majority of their productive time talking about the past. Instead, one very common thing about successful people is their refusal to allow the past dictate the heights they will reach in life.

If you have that great desire to be financially free and wealthy in life, you must firstly agree within yourself that your past cannot in anyway determine where you will get to in life. The past simply does not matter. This is very important because it is the matter of the mind. A man who does not deal with such issue at the early part of his life may live to regret his existence. The end point of such a man was defined by Haruki Murakami in the famous: *Dance, Dance, Dance,* where he puts it like this, "Unfortunately, the clock is ticking, and the hours are going by. The past increases, the future recedes. Possibilities decreasing, regrets mounting."

CHAPTER FOUR

THE WRONG WAY!

We have confirmed that having money is a very good thing! Money answers all things, money opens and closes doors. Having abundance of money gives you the best comfort you can ever imagine in life. Being wealthy means that you rarely have anything to lack in your life. All these and many more benefits of having abundance of wealth are important and very attractive, In fact, nothing is juicier.

However, many people often look for money in the wrong ways, yeah! The total wrong way. I could remember a long time ago when I was very young, my friends and I would always gist and dream about travelling to the United States of America. Our dreams of travelling to the U.S were so big and giant! We literarily often told our parents that once we finished high school, we would find our ways into the bird-like structure in the sky and we would fly down into one of the big cities of the good people of America. We were desperate! We wanted to experience life in California and New York without even considering whatever we were going to do to get there - either it's a good thing or a bad one. Do you know why we were having this fantasies and dreams? The sole reason was because we read a tale that money grows on the trees there. As funny as it looks, that was exactly our motive for wanting to travel down to the United States. I guess we all believe that it is not true, we were being tricked into believing the inexistence, and because we were desperate for the wrong reasons and didn't mind whatever it would cost us, things didn't work out.

Some people who desire to be wealthy often want to have abundance of money using shortcuts. They often forget that no one gets to the very top ladder of success and great wealth without hard work. Margaret Thatcher puts it like this, "I do not know anyone who has got to the top without hard work. That is the recipe, It will not always get you to the top but it should get you pretty close."

Many young people in our world today are

after the good things of life in the wrong way.

Those who are desperate and do not have the intention to make wealth in the right way are prone to getting engaged in fraudulent, scandalous and questionable acts. They are the sort of people who will go any length to acquire wealth.

Taking a good look at arm robbers, prostitutes and other category of people who perfectly fit into this description, they do not care about what it is going to cost them in order to have wealth. Those who can assassinate in order to have money in abundance are following the wrong way, People who can offer their body in order to be wealthy are not following the right way. I do not think there is a two way to this.

Another category of people who are not on the right path to having wealth are the ones who have very poor mindsets about wealth. They are the sort of people who do not believe that they can become rich and wealthy because of their background and education. They have allowed their backgrounds to pull their backs to the ground. You will agree with me that this sort of mentality is like a road that leads to penury.

CHAPTER FIVE

WHAT YOU NEED TO BECOME FINANCIALLY FREE IS WITHIN YOU

You have the potential to become financially free and wealthy in life. You do not need to neither go there nor here because all that you need is within you. Many people often make the mistake of chasing businesses, seminars, trainings and events that do not in anyway align to their God given potential. This is simply like chasing the wind.

Jim Rohn once said, "The big challenge is to become all that you have the possibility of becoming, you cannot believe what it does to the human spirit to maximize your human potential and stretch yourself to the limit." Lack of desire to look inward, discover what you really carry - in terms of your potentials - and maximizing them to the fullest are the major reason why lots of folks are still tied down to the poor financial conditions they have found themselves.

It is such a common occurrence that many

people look at others while they ought to look at themselves. Instead of envying the success of others due to your own failure in your career or business, it is important that you truly look inward and realize what makes you unique and that you can offer to people; who in return are ever ready to go all out to pay you for who you are and what you do. In the words of Stewart Johnson, "Our business in life is not to get ahead of others, but to get ahead of ourselves - to break our own records, to outstrip our yesterdays by today, to do our work with more force than diligence."

In one of his books, John Mason once highlighted, "If you would like to know who is responsible for most of your troubles, take a look at yourself in the mirror. If you could kick the fellow responsible for most of your problems, you wouldn't be able to sit down for three weeks." This corroborates the fact that why you haven't become financially free is simply because of what you haven't done yet or because of what you have done. If you have figured out your potentials and utilized them judiciously, you would probably have become a young billionaire today. If you do not figure out your potentials and maximized them for profit making, then you are not ready to have money in abundance. As young as Mark Zuckerberg was when he founded Facebook while studying at Harvard University, he was able to discover his potentials and has continued to maximize them to the fullest. Mark Zuckerberg, today, remains one of the youngest billionaire in the whole wide world.

Do not make the mistake of being satisfied and relaxed because you are busy working, even though what you earn is as little as the dust in the sky. If you truly know the worth of the potentials embedded inside of you, you will go all out to make great use of them in order to become financially free and wealthy. I love the words John Mason here: "Everyone is on the move. People are moving forward, backward, and sometimes nowhere at all as though they are on a treadmill. The mistake most people make is thinking that the main goal of life is to stay busy. Such thinking is a trap. What is important is not whether you are busy, but whether you are progressing. The question is one of activity versus accomplishment." Form the habit of utilizing your potentials in a progressive way. You will certainly be amazed at how big you will grow in no distant time. All you need is within you!

CHAPTER SIX

ALWAYS APPLY THE PRINCIPLES OF SUCCESSFUL PEOPLE

Now, you would ask who the successful people are? Successful people are those who daily live in the abundance of wealth all their lives. They are people who have gone through the thick, thin, rough perches and have discovered what it truly takes to be wealthy. Due to the mistakes they made along the way, the lessons they learnt along the way, and the various experiences they have been able to gather along the path of poverty and the path of wealth. They have principles which anyone who desires to become wealthy and successful in life can study and apply into their careers and businesses. In order to become financially free and wealthy, it is important to apply the principles of successful people. By the time you begin to apply them, all the factors around you will begin to work in line with your vision of becoming financially free in life, despite whatever struggle or problem you might be passing through.

Many people are stagnant in their pursuit of abundance of money because they have refused to unlearn and relearn. They are often ignorant that without changing and following the blueprints of successful people, becoming financially free will continue to be a mirage in their lives. Charles Darwin, the father of evolution puts it like this, "It is not the strongest of the species that survive, nor the most intelligent, but the one most responsive to change. To Norman Vincent Peale, it's simply like this: "Change your thoughts and you change your world." Without changing your thoughts and feeding your mind with principles and ideologies of successful people, it is nearly impossible to become financially free.

In your business and career, just take a critical look at those who are flying high in the sky of great abundance of wealth; take a good look at the principles guiding their lives, this is key to becoming wealthy like them. Perhaps there are certain routines they engage in that the average person in your niche or field of endeavour do not take proper look at. Their dedication to work or business might be second to none. The hours they spend in a day on productive activities that brings more money into their accounts might be different from that of you and others. Overall, the principles- both large and little - that have made these set of people to become wealthy and successful in a similar endeavour are the crucial ones that you need to critically take a look at and apply into your own career or business.

Always remember, humbling yourself to learn principles from successful people will save you years that it will normally take you to learn them on your own. Instead of listening to negative people and their usual 'you cannot do it' draining talks, it much more advantageous to feed on books, tapes, pod cast and video authored by successful people. Rich Mayo dropped this valuable lines sometimes ago, "You've got to be careful whom you pattern yourself after, because you are likely to become exactly like them." So, I ask you: Would you rather learn principles of success and wealth or listen to the words of negative people?

CONCLUSION

Becoming financially free and wealthy is not a mirage, despite your background, education or the present challenges facing you in life.

All the potentials mentioned that will help you to become great in life are embedded inside of you. You just need to make a decision at the beginning of your life and career that you want to be financially free.

Refuse to be lazy and ordinary in your endeavours.

Make the decision to become rich and do all your possible best to ensure that you become rich. Always remember that there is no substitute for HARDWORK. Every successful people are hardworking people.

Do not wait to listen to people who tell you that your goal is impossible and that you cannot be what you desire to become.

By the time you put all these into practice, you will be amazed at how all the factors around you begin to help you to achieve your dream of becoming the next big billionaire!